About

This all began one Saturday morning. I wanted to surprise
my daughter with something new for breakfast. So, inspired
by something I saw once before, I began to play around with
drawing on my griddle. They started out a little weird, but
after a couple failed attempts and timing experiments'
... BAM. I was ready!

I called my daughter to the breakfast counter and presented
her with a pancake in the shape of the famous Mouse. Instantly,
I saw her eyes light up with sheer joy. This is a memory I will never
forget. However, little did I know, this successful attempt would
become a weekend tradition. My daughter began to challenge
me with the impossible. Whether it was a Unicorn with a long
magical horn, or a character from that cartoon, I continued to
make her imaginings become tasty morning treats. I was her hero.

Hi, I'm Big Daddy, a single father who enjoys making creative and
healthy meals for my family. There is nothing better than being
able to put a smile on my kid's face. Isn't that what life is all about?
So, I decided to create a cookbook to help others become kitchen
heroes. I worked on many techniques and tried a few different
batters – the best results are in this book to hopefully help and
guide you every step of the way. Your technique and style will only
improve with practice, so always keep trying and never give up.
Also, don't be scared to mess up, you can eat your mistakes. :)
More importantly, this is a great chance for you to capture lasting
memories with your child. Trust me, they will never forget.

Make someone special smile, everyday.

How to Create Pancake Shapes
Zoo Animal & Holiday Edition
Volume 1

Written & Illustrated
by Paul Kaiser

Big Daddy Pancakes

Equipment

6

Pantry

7

Recipe

9

Technique

10, 11

Dash

15

Flash

16

Lucky

17

Huggy

18

Roary

19

Waddles

21

Izzy

22

Gabby

23

Cheeky

24

Vixen

25

Kermit

26

Speedy

27

More Friends

28

29

Rudolph

33

Mittens

34

Snowflakes

35

Trees

36

Holly

37

Gingy

38

Starry

40

Snow Globe

40

Angel

40

Sleigh

40

Candy Cane

41

Ornament

42

Lights

43

Frosty

44

Wreath

45

Claus

47

Tips & Tricks

48

Notes

50

For more techniques and videos,
check often below at:

www.bigdaddypancakes.com

Equipment

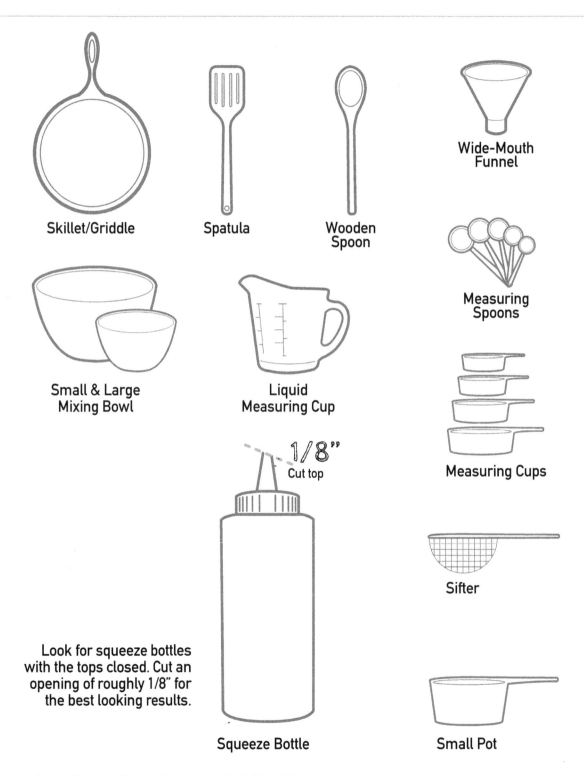

Skillet/Griddle

Spatula

Wooden Spoon

Wide-Mouth Funnel

Measuring Spoons

Small & Large Mixing Bowl

Liquid Measuring Cup

Measuring Cups

1/8"
Cut top

Sifter

Look for squeeze bottles with the tops closed. Cut an opening of roughly 1/8" for the best looking results.

Squeeze Bottle

Small Pot

Pantry

All-Purpose Flour

Baking Soda

Baking Powder

Sugar

Salt

extra flavor

Nutmeg

Cinnamon

Pumpkin Spice

The WET Ingredients

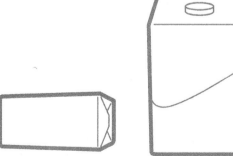

Unsalted Butter

Buttermilk

Vanilla Extract

Large Eggs

Basic
Recipe

Creates roughly
8 characters

Step ONE - DRY Ingredients

Sift the following ingredients through a sifter, into a large bowl.

- ○ 2 cup   All-Purpose Flour
- ○ 2 TB   Baking Soda
- ○ 2 TB   Baking Powder
- ○ 2 TB   Sugar
- ○ Pinch   Salt

Add a little spice in your mix, try one, (or all) of these.
Sometimes adding a little extra flavor can add to the season.

- ○ 1/4 tsp Nutmeg
- ○ 1/4 tsp Cinnamon
- ○ 1/4 tsp Pumpkin Spice

Step TWO - WET Ingredients

Melt the butter in a small pot. Allow it to cool a few minutes, then combine in a bowl with buttermilk and vanilla.

- ○ 2 TB   Unsalted Butter
- ○ 2+1/4 cup   Buttermilk
- ○ 2 TB   Vanilla Extract

Crack the eggs into the large bowl with the DRY ingredients

- ○ 2 lrg   Eggs

After many recipes, we enjoyed this basic one the most. You can always use any batter or box version if you choose.

It's time to get creative and have fun!

Step THREE

Pour the WET ingredients into the large mixing bowl of DRY ingredients. Fold the mixture together with a wooden spoon. If the batter is too thick, add 1 TB Milk until the consistency is just right and smooth. Then, pour the batter into the squeeze bottles. This can be done carefully without a funnel, but using one may help.

- ○ Fold, Stir & Create

Griddle Techniques

The Line Squeeze

To make precise lines consistently, use a bottle with a small 1/8" opening. This size helps to define the shape as the heat cooks the batter. You don't need to go fast with your lines – nice steady, slow, clean lines do the job.

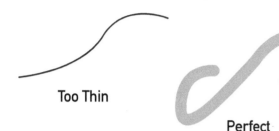

Too Thin

Perfect

Too Thick

Remember, the batter will expand as it cooks.

Follow The Lines

The dotted lines show what to do during each step along the way.

The Process

Pour the batter to fill the large areas. To add a unique touch to your masterpiece, leave some of the areas like the eyes, nose and mouth open.

Draw

Cover

Flip

In order for your design to hold its shape and look nice, you must give the batter time to cook and set to a deeper color. We found 30 seconds to be a good rule. You can adjust timing based on the temperature of your griddle.

The average pancake is about 7" in diameter. So think about the size of your space ahead of time and realize how big you want to make your character. It will take a few tries to get used to how far apart to keep the features. Once you master the distance, it will be more simple and fun than a plain circle pancake.

ZOO
Animals

Dash
Flash
Lucky
Huggy
Roary
Waddles
Izzy
Gabby
Cheeky
Vixen
Kermit
Speedy
Tiny
Hooty
Sunshine
Albert
Slim
Bully
Oscar
Dory

Dash

Loyal. Kind. Everyone's best friend.
You will fall in love with him from the
first hug. He will always be at your side.
This quick little pooch is the best there is.

Difficulty: Medium

Step ONE

**Eyes, Nose
& Whisker Dots.**

Step TWO

Face, Ears & Spots.

(Connecting the ears to
face helps you flip later.)

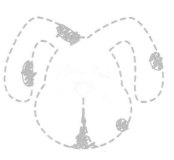

WAIT 30 SEC

Step THREE

**Fill. Leave Eyes
& Nose Open.**

Step FOUR

Flip & Reveal.

Doggy Bowl

(Add small chocolate chips for food)

Step ONE

Step DONE

Dog Treats

Step ONE

Step DONE

Flash

Quick. Witty. Hungry for more.
This rabbit loves to nibble on carrots
and run around any garden.

Difficulty: Medium

Step
ONE

**Eyes, Nose,
Whiskers & Dots.**

Step
TWO

Face & Ears.

WAIT SEC

Step
THREE

**Fill. Leave Eyes
& Nose Open.**

Step
FOUR

Flip & Reveal.

Carrot Treat

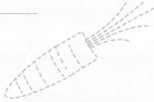

Step ONE

Step DONE

Lucky

Cuddly. Fun. Playful for hours.
A cat named Lucky must have 9 lives.
Our cat sure uses them all.

Difficulty: Medium

Step
ONE

Eyes & Nose.

Step
TWO

Face, Tongue, Ears
& Long Whiskers.

WAIT 30 SEC

Step
THREE

Fill. Leave Eyes
& Nose Open.

Step
FOUR

Flip & Reveal.

Fishy Treat

(Add a small chocolate chip for eye.)

Step ONE   Step DONE

Ball of Yarn

Step ONE   Step DONE

Huggy

Warm. Loving. Ready for a winter nap.
Every bear enjoys grabbing a fish by
the river before a snooze.

Difficulty: Easy

Step
ONE

Eyes & Nose.

Step
TWO

Face & Ears.

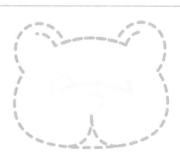

WAIT **30** SEC

Step
THREE

Fill. Leave Eyes
& Nose Open.

Step
FOUR

Flip & Reveal.

Pillow

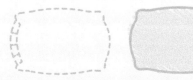

Step ONE   Step DONE

Bear Treats

(Add a small chocolate chip for eye or sprinkles for body.)

Step ONE   Step DONE

Roary

Loud. Fluffy. Ready for the circus. Before the show he is about to put on for the crowd, this lion is hungry for his meal.

Difficulty: Hard

Step ONE
Eyes, Nose & Ears.

Step TWO
Face & Mane.

WAIT

Step THREE
Fill. Leave Eyes & Nose Open.

Step FOUR
Flip & Reveal.

Steak Treats

Step ONE

Step DONE

Circus Hoop

Step ONE

Step DONE

19

Waddles

Fun. Cute. A curly tail of happiness.
This farm animal loves to play in the mud and makes
sure to save his piggy pennies for a rainy day.

Difficulty: Easy

Step ONE

Eyes & Snout.

Step TWO

Face & Ears.

WAIT 30 SEC

Step THREE

Fill. Leave Eyes
& Nose Open.

Step FOUR

Flip & Reveal.

Dirty Trough

(Add small chocolate chips for food.)

Step ONE

Step DONE

Piggy Bank

Step ONE

Step DONE

Izzy

Kind. Sweet. Pecking with love.
This chick enjoys a simple meal and
surrounding herself with loved ones.

Difficulty: Easy

Step
ONE

Eyes & Beak.

Step
TWO

Head & Tuft
of Hair.

WAIT **30** SEC

Step
THREE

Fill Entire Head.

Step
FOUR

Flip & Reveal.

Chick Feet Tracks

Step ONE

Step DONE

Chick Feed

(Add small chocolate chips for food.)

Step ONE

Step DONE

Gabby

Warm. Loving. Loves leafy treats.
Reaching high with a tall giraffe neck,
this one always shares with her family.

Difficulty: Hard

Step ONE

Eyes & Nose.

Step TWO

Face. Ears.
Horns & Spots.
(Creating the horns
separately can help
you flip later.)

WAIT 30 SEC

Step THREE

Fill. Leave
Eyes Open.

Step FOUR

Flip & Reveal.
(Tuck horns under head.)

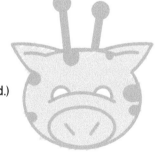

Leafy Eats

Step ONE

Step DONE

Cheeky

Silly. Scratchy. Banana crazy.
Don't look away, because this little
monkey loves to play with his food.

Difficulty: Easy

Step ONE

Eyes. Nose
& Wide Mouth.

Step TWO

Face & Ears.

WAIT **30** SEC

Step THREE

Fill. Leave
Mouth Open.

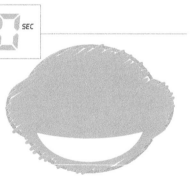

Step FOUR

Flip & Reveal.

Banana Treat

Step ONE

Step DONE

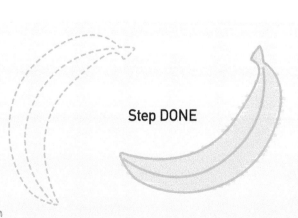

Vixen

Sneaky. Loving. Ready for a winter run.
Only one animal can outwit anyone on it's
tail by it's quick feet and foxy smarts.

Difficulty: Medium

Step ONE
Eyes & Nose.

Step TWO
Face & Ears.

WAIT **30** SEC

Step THREE
Fill & Leave
Nose Open.

Step FOUR
Flip & Reveal.

Foxes Tail

Step ONE

Step DONE

Hiding in the Leaves

Step ONE

Step DONE

Kermit

Happy. Hopping fun. Always hungry.
This froggy keeps life simple,
leaping from one lily pad to the
other to get his meal.

Difficulty: Easy

Step ONE

Eyes & Mouth.

Step TWO

Entire Head.

WAIT **30** SEC

Step THREE

**Fill. Leave
Eyes Open.**

Step FOUR

Flip & Reveal.

Buggy Treat

Step ONE

Step DONE

Lily Pad

Step ONE

Step DONE

How to Create Pancake Shapes: Zoo Animal & Holiday Edition

Speedy

Slow.Winner. A patient friend.
This little one knows life is a marathon
and takes his time to any finish line.

Difficulty: Hard

Step ONE

Eyes, Mouth
& Body.

Step TWO

Eyes & Shell.

WAIT **30** SEC

Step THREE

Fill Body & Shell.

Step FOUR

Flip & Reveal.

Leafy Eats

Step ONE

Step DONE

27

More Friends

Tiny
Slither
Slide.

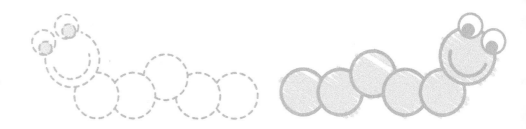

Whooty
Magical Watch Bird.
Flying with Grace.

Sunshine
Blue Skies.
Perfect Days.

Albert
Never Forgets.
Loves Peanuts.

Slim

Big.
Slow & Lovable.

Bully

Adventurous
Bulky.

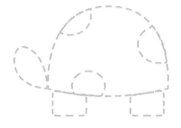 

Oscar

Courageous
Nimble.

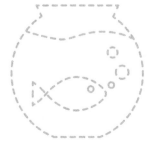 

Dory

Bubbles.
Bubbles.
Bubbles.

Enjoy the
HOLIDAY

Rudolph

Mittens

Snowflakes

Trees

Holly

Gingy

Starry

Snow globe

Angel

Sleigh

Candy Cane

Ornament

Lights

Frosty

Wreath

Claus

Rudolph

Leading the pack with a bright light.
Anytime you see him, he's on his reindeer way
to deliver special gifts to all boys & girls.

Difficulty: Medium

Step
ONE

Eyes & Nose.

WAIT **30** SEC

Step
TWO

Head & Antlers.

(Creating the antlers
separately can help
you flip later.)

Step
THREE

Fill. Leave Eyes Open.

Step
FOUR

Flip & Reveal.

(Tuck antlers under head.)

Add a Shiny Red Nose

Add a simple touch by separating some batter in a different bowl and adding red food
coloring. You can fill the nose with this new batter or make a new shape and put the
bright and shiny nose right on the top.

Mittens

Brrrr. It's cold outside. You can't make a snowman without covering you hands.

Difficulty: Medium

Step ONE

Cuffs & String.

(You can make the mittens & string separate, then attach later

Step TWO

Both Mittens.

WAIT **30** SEC

Step THREE

Fill.

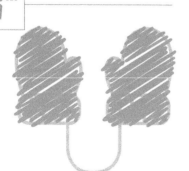

Step FOUR

Flip & Reveal.

Snowball Fight

Traditional pancakes are nothing more than snowballs! Make a few and add gloves.

Flakes

No two snowflakes are the same. No matter the shape, you'll love catching these on your tongue.

Difficulty: Easy

ONE

Criss Cross.

TWO

Endless Circles.

THREE

Chicken Feet.

FOUR

Starry Night.

Trees

Ornaments. Lights.
Every tree is special.
What makes yours unique?

Difficulty: Easy

Step ONE

Tree Sections

Step TWO

Ornaments & Topper.

WAIT **30** SEC

Step THREE

Fill completely.

Step FOUR

Flip & Reveal.

Shiny Star

Top off this tree with a bright star

Step ONE

Step DONE

Holly

Festive. Tradition.
Fills everyone's hearts with cheer.

Difficulty: Easy

Step ONE

Berries.

(Make the berries separate and attach later.)

Step TWO

Leaves.

WAIT 30 SEC

Step THREE

Fill.

Step FOUR

Flip & Reveal.

(Tuck leaves under berries.)

Red Berries & Green Leaves

Add a simple touch by mixing red food coloring and batter in a different bowl. Make tiny drops for berries. Add green coloring to a different bowl of batter and put in a squeeze bottle to shape the leaves.

Gingy

Sweet. Joyful. A fun holiday companion.
This season, no one can resist this little man's
happy smile and yummy buttons.

Difficulty: Easy

Step
ONE

Eyes, Mouth
& Buttons.

Step
TWO

Body.

WAIT

Step
THREE

Fill. Leave Eyes,
Mouth & Buttons Open.

Step
FOUR

Flip & Reveal.

Belly Full of Fun

Decorate with a few little pieces of multi-colored candy to make Gingy extra festive.

More Holidays

Starry

Shiny.
Bright.

Snow Globe

Magical.
Filled with Joy.

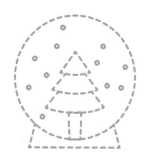 

Angel

Beautiful.
Watching Over.

Sleigh

Santa's Favorite.
Delivery Service.

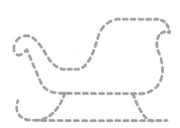 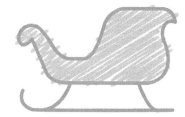

Candy Canes

Striped. Classic.
There's no better sweet than a
candy cane hanging on your tree.

Difficulty: Easy

Step
ONE

Canes.

Step
TWO

Stripes.

WAIT **30** SEC

Step
THREE

Fill.

Step
FOUR

Flip & Reveal.

Red & Green Stripes

Add a simple touch by using red and green food coloring in different bowls mixed with batter.
Fill bottles to draw the outline and stripes inside the candy cane in contrasting colors.

Ornament

New. Old. Happy reminders.
No matter the shape, you look forward
to seeing them on your tree every year.

Difficulty: Medium

Step ONE

Ornament Body.

Step TWO

Top & Pattern.

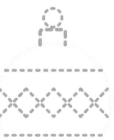

WAIT **30** SEC

Step THREE

Fill.

Step FOUR

Flip & Reveal.

Ornament Color Variations

Add a simple touch by using other food coloring options and mixing them with
batter in separate bowls. Fill squeeze bottles and then draw fun and colorful patterns
inside the ornament.

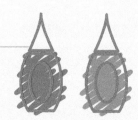

Lights

Merry. Bright.
Fill any room with warm color
and light up every night.

Difficulty: Medium

Step
ONE

String.

Step
TWO

Light bulbs.

WAIT

Step
THREE

Fill.

Step
FOUR

Flip & Reveal.

Multi-Colored Lights

Try creating a variety of colors on your strand of lights by mixing food
coloring with batter in separate bowls. Then fill squeeze bottles and use
to fill in the outlined lights.

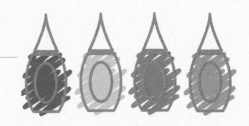

Frosty

Rolled with love.
Created with excitement.
Makes every passerby smile.

Difficulty: Medium

Step
ONE

Body & Arms.

Step
TWO

**Buttons & Eyes.
Carrot Nose.**

WAIT **30** SEC

Step
THREE

Fill completely

Step
FOUR

Flip & Reveal

Top Hat

Have Frosty come to life with a magical top hat.

Step ONE

Step DONE

 How to Create Pancake Shapes: Zoo Animals & Holiday Edition

Wreath

Decorating doors. Bringing cheer.
Brighten the season and
make your festive.

Difficulty: Medium

Step ONE

Bow.

(Make the bow separately
and attach later.)

Step TWO

Wreath & Berries.

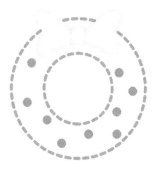

WAIT SEC

Step THREE

Fill.

Step FOUR

Flip & Reveal.

Sweet Berries

A few little pieces of red candies add a festive treat to this holiday wreath.

Claus

Making a list. Checking it twice.
This jolly old soul shares gifts with the world and brings
smiles to children, in days past and for years to come.

Difficulty: Medium

Step ONE

Hat.

Step TWO

Eyes, Mouth,
Beard & Face.

WAIT

Step THREE

Fill the Hat & Beard.

Step FOUR

Flip & Reveal.

Add a Shiny Red Hat

Try mixing red food coloring and batter in an individual bowl
– then use this batter to draw and make a stocking for Santa!

Step ONE   Step DONE

Tips & Tricks

Make Extras

Make an extra batch and store it in the freezer. This prepares for last-minute breakfast ideas. Make-ahead meals are always a great option when you want to enjoy breakfast with your family or on the run.

Reheat in the toaster for the best results.

Warm Oven

At the lowest setting, place a cookie sheet in the oven. When a few pancakes are done, place them on the sheet to keep them warm while you keep making more pancakes.

Don't keep them in the oven too long as they will dry out. 15 minutes max.

Add Color

Use this tip when you want to get creative and really impress your crowd. Separate into different bowls. Add a few drops of food coloring, then bottle it up and use in your design. The results are amazing when you try more than one color. This is fun to do after you get your basic technique down. Imagine creating a colorful rainbow on a rainy day for your munchkin.

Make Ahead

If you think the next day will be hectic in the morning, your batter can be made the night before.. Store it in the refrigerator, either in the squeeze bottles or in a bowl. You'll need to let the batter come to room temp (approx. 15/20 minutes) before getting to work. With any batter, the results are best right after mixing, as all the active ingredients react to the to griddle slightly better. This doesn't affect the flavor at all, but it will save you time in the morning.

Add Flavor

If you want to switch up your syrup for another treat, try spreading a few other options instead. Jam. Jelly. Chocolate spread. Peanut butter. Marshmallow spread. Even cut up fruit is enough to give your pancakes a twist of flavor.

Notes

How to Create Pancake Shapes: Zoo Animal & Holiday Edition

This book is dedicated to my daughters,
Isabella & Gabriella. I Love You!

Big Daddy

Look for more Big Daddy Pancakes cookbooks!
For more techniques & videos, check out:

www.bigdaddypancakes.com